## Sara Kestelman

trained at the Central School of
Drama and has worked in
theatre, including the dual role of Titania and
Hippolyta in Peter Brook's RSC production of
*A Midsummer Night's Dream* and as Rosalind in
*As You Like It* at the National Theatre. She has
just completed *Three Tall Women* with Maggie
Smith and Samantha Bond. Her films include
Boorman's *Zardoz*, Ken Russell's *Listomania*
and on television she recently played the part
of Queenie Leavis in BBC Screen 2's *The Last
Romantics*.

## Susan Penhaligon

is best known for her television and film work,
including her role as Pru in *A Bouquet Of Barbed
Wire* and as Judi Dench's sister in *A Fine
Romance*. Her films include the cult thriller
*Patrick*, Paul Verhoven's *Survival Run* and the
part of Mae Rose Cottage in *Under Milk Wood*.
She first worked with Sara Kestelman in the
theatrical production of *Three Sisters*, and her
other stage credits include Stoppard's *The Real
Thing*, Dunyasha in *The Cherry Orchard*, and
Olwyn Peel in *Dangerous Corner* at the
Whitehall Theatre.

Central. June 2009

For Audrey —
love
Sara x

# A TWO HANDER

## Sara Kestelman &
## Susan Penhaligon

*Sara Kestelman*

THE DO-NOT
PRESS

This collection first Published in Great Britain in 1996 by
The Do-Not Press
PO Box 4215
London SE23 2QD

A Paperback Original

Collection copyright © 1996 by The Do-Not Press
Individual poems © 1996 by Sara Kestelman & Susan Penhaligon
All rights reserved

ISBN 1 89934 08 X

Printed and bound in Great Britain by The Guernsey Press Co Ltd,
Guernsey, Channel Islands

# Contents

\

*For Richie*

## *Film Star*

I showed my body when I was young
like a dog at Crufts.
Forgetting my art, I posed,
my nipples wet-nosed,
with gartered legs and
pouting lips
shamelessly I wagged my tail.

Now I am older these images re-print
to haunt me
although I'm changed
and doodles have appeared around
my eyes,
I am set in plaster
like starry hands
on Hollywood Boulevard,
forever juicy
forever wanting
forever peachy.

# Heart

'Where do you live?'
   he said,
'In my heart,'
   she said.

'Is it light?'
   he said,
'It's large,'
   she said.

'Is it bright?'
   he said,
'It has glass,'
   she said,
'but some of the panes got smashed,
some are still boarded up,
so, were you to visit just now
it might seem a little bit dim –
but I hope by the spring
all will be right
and gleaming bright again.

Perhaps you will visit me then?'

## To Alcohol

A sullen mute lived
courteously between us
fearing the chop at
any time

And come summer,
when the mock orange tree
bloomed,
I called his bluff,
and left.

## *Looping The Hoop*

'You shouldn't always wear black',
she said,
'you ought to display yourself more,
change your hair,
pierce your ears,
wear some big silver hoops –
trust me, you'll love it I'm sure!'

So I first pierced my ears
here in Bristol
twenty-one years ago;
my girlfriend insisted that I should
and it was only because
I promised I would
that I didn't just turn tail and go.

The lady I went to botched it
in a crowded back room of a store;
one ear perfect, the other off centre
so my brand new surprise Gypsy hoops
– my friend's prize –
dangled asymmetric
and askew.

I evened it up two years later
with a tiny diamond stud;
I kept it there twinkling in the lobe of my ear
until September of this very year
when Fate and mixed fortune
involved my return
and I lost it
right here in Bristol.

## *To the Critic*

I hope you burn in oil
and your lips turn inside out,
I hope you get varicose veins
that travel down your nose.
I wish I was your dentist
I'd find the nerve, as you have found with me,
and slowly put the needle through your teeth.
I hope you fall full-faced into a pile of dung,
as you said I did.

I hope your hair drops out
and all the boys you fancy
turn into frogs,
I hope you bang into a plank of wood,
then you would know how coarse the grain was,
and worst of all,
I wish you as a critic to criticise yourself
and suffer a plague of useless metaphors
tarring and feathering your reputation.

## Observation

Easy over, over easy
lovely lazy golden hand
trailing through gleaming azure
shimmering over sun bleached sand;
and if you're right,
dear friend,
in fearing that the inevitable end –
the biggest bang of all –
is so very close at hand,
what possible harm
could there be then
in taking time to celebrate
the beauty of your arm?

## Land Locked

I could cry for a view of the sea,
the mere thought of a bit of surf
crashing onto Porthmeor beach
makes me ache.
Any water would do,
although the colours of the Thames
don't quite shock me into acquiescence
and the English channel on a grey day is drear.
There are those lakes near Reading,
but they don't do much,
the herons idly beaking at the inky edge.

I suppose it's Cornish sea I miss,
the blue, blue billow of waves
that salivate across the sea gulled rocks
by cushion grass coated in pinks
where once I walked
when unashamedly so little
and easily persuaded

## Scenes From a Sea-Side Chalet

One forty-five in the morning
standing on South Shields beach;
a crescent moon hanging low
shrouded in cloud
throwing
a hazy waxen glow
over the ink black sea.

Halloween, late october;
the silver surf rolling in strips –
perfect sharp parallel lines
crisp white light, fluorescent bright
zippering salt to sand,
peeling out along the way
past Lizard Point
from Souter Lighthouse and Roker Bay
to Sunderland and beyond.

# *Wanted*

St. Ives
sticky in the sixties,
bohemians
spatchcock in the sun.
On the harbour beach
artists,
paint streaked arteries,
(too much vino veritas),
smell of unwashed hair,
turps and surfing beards
swaggering in the sea.

Naked
nomadic, leather thonged
sloppy jumpered artists,
voluptuous,
in the lusty, bedable summer air.
On the brink,
the tip
of this quixotic land,
the rim
the perimeter of life,
dragooned for their
quiet revolution.

And I,
a fatherless girl
held aloft by burnished arms,
held and healed and cherished
and included.

# Ode To A Rake

Should you someday hear, my dearest Rake,
that I am gone –
grieve not,
but remember on
and of a long hot summer:
some plays, some art, Costello, clowns, a dish of tea,
a bowl of steaming mussels,
yes, remember me;
gentle swell of the canal,
hubbub above, peace below
a ting-a-ling ride from the box PO,
sharing a poem and a line or two;
the sweet & funny rock 'n' roll of you;
the delight, the folly, 'Maggie', 'Molly',
narrow wooden world tucked away
under the willow & the concrete of Westway.
Great craic!
Yes, remember me
and keep track, dear Poet Rake,
of all the different lines we've drawn
and someday,
typewriter upon your knee,
weave them into the fabric
of a really good story.
Make no mistake, Rake dear,
you have the eye,
you have the ear
so mazeltov dear one,
and rock on doll, rock on !

## An Old Man

When I was fourteen I met Robert Graves –
it seemed nothing
to watch him naked
dive like a Baccus
into the sea
in Deja
in the sun.

One day a finger pointed straight at me –
you'll never be an actress
stay here
be Spanish
learn to make
good dressing
for the salad.

I thought him damning and presumptuous
under the olive trees –
and wretchedly
grew small
beside his regal Roman face.

To be fourteen is difficult enough
without having some poet
pushing your face in the paella.

## *Cabaret*

The Dream –
     when you're young –
is as big as it needs to be,
stretching limitless
out and beyond –
brilliant
shimmering bright.

As a child
I stood upon mine
unaware
of where I was;
it lay beneath me
blindingly white
with a sound –
     not loud at all
     but pitched unnaturally high –
emanating from
deep within
the convex sandscape
I stood upon.

Yet
Somehow
I never got inside
my dream,
and older now
it shrinks
bit by bit
to the circumference of arms
shortly to balance
football size
on the centre of one palm...

I wonder,
will I dare
to chuck it in the air
and catch it?
Or will I lift my boot
and give it a hefty kick
to kingdom come?...
Well,
life is a Cabaret old chum…

## *How To Be Successful*

And when the bolshi stars come down and touch you
the dust will sharpen in the affecting sun
glinting on your forehead –
well spotted by those who give the breaks.
In innocence, they do not know why
you seem so specially glowing –
but for the star dust
of course you wouldn't be.

## Day Tripper

Man in St Ives
nose against gallery window
called his wife,
don't bother looking
it's only paintings.

## Summer of '73

It was a summer, the summer of '73;
they met at the lunch of a mutual friend,
and later he most generously
helped fix the cheap mail-order chair –
which ought to have been sent back
but is there still rocking in her kitchen.
The year of "A Touch Of Class"
and "King Marvin's Garden"
which he,
or so the diary says,
was more moved by than she...

Work then took her away to Ireland – a two month stay.
He wrote beautiful cards to her there
(found in a box only last year);
and in Dublin she bought the crocodile shoes,
platforms,
with delicate straps buckled loose
and the ever so high high-heels,
and wound round her ankle the little chain
that would from that time forever remain.

She wore them for him with a petal flared skirt
when they re-met in London on that last date,
the night before she packed up her bags
back on her travels again.
Much later he told her she'd hurt him then;
Miss head-in-the-air, head elsewhere –
speckled, freckled flutter-by, butterfly
heading off to Bristol...

What followed remains a mystery.
But in Bristol it was that he lost her,
the late summer of '73.

## *The Flame*

My son,
you grow like a burning torch
all eager, bright and whiteness
from your hair,
and your life reaches out
burns and traps me
grinning with love
I fed you from my breast,
burning bright no pain for you,
no loss of will or sordid stuff,
all believing in your life
like the Olympic flame.

## Homesick for Africa – from a report in the newspaper.

I built my hut
from the earth of Dagenham
at the end of my garden.
The mud pies
carefully moulded
as my mother taught
grew high and round like a tower
and I,
my melancholy eased
sang tribal songs
blinded to the shocked eyes
of neighbours
their gardens cucumber green
and sliced so thinly
beside my earthen folly.
Perhaps they could not smile
as I,
to see the heat of Africa
cooling in an English afternoon.

But then the council came
just as my paint
had dried azure as a Cameroon sky,
my hut was not allowed
as if I did not know
and only wooden sheds would do.
I must destroy my home
and learn the ways of Essex,
a colonialist from the council said.

So now I stand
before my half demolished den
staring at you
in your suburbs
from a photo in the newspaper
with a wordless cry.
You can see my confusion
for surely this dark earth
belongs to all of us?

## *Christmas Carol*

Hey you!
with the softlips!
you –
yes, you
of the early night
and the measured measure
of vintage scotch –
you
of the cashmered elbow
pressed into
brocade and chintz
overlooking
Hyde Park
on the second day
of a new year –
I just wanna say
thankyou!

# A Wanting

What a mean wizard Merlin is
forgetting to put you in my bed today,
love-sick, I taunt him for his laziness.

And I, stretched star shaped on the warm earth,
licking my fingers in the busy air with bees,
hot like a summer sun in August,

try summoning his magic
to make you suddenly appear.

# Conundrums

How to fight
inertia
when inertia
robs the fight –
a conundrum;
how is it possible
to have a corner
to a ring –
well,
take a long strong
spring out from it,
o'er leap
the ropes confining it
and so
release
and separate
the circle from the
square.
Perhaps the key lies there.

## Bearded Lady

Beneath the clock tower sits
the bearded lady of Leatherhead,
counting the hairs on her chin
in solemn wonderment
at her own uniqueness.

Her cherry-redded lips are grim
as she speaks the numbers of her awe –
to shave or not to shave
that is the question,
and thus succumbing to reason,
be beardless.

Beneath the clock tower sits
the bearded lady of Leatherhead
loud hailing her hirsuteness,
her heavy leaded eyes are dim
as she surveys the laughing world –

and people pass
and people stare,
her frilly dress
her curly hair,
she doesn't care
she doesn't care.

## Golden Boy

A perfect English summer's day
brings you
and the gleaming ray of sunshine you beam
through the darker aspects of you –
into unexpected focus.

And I wonder –
do you know
that the sweetness of you,
Golden Boy,
touches very deep?

## *Happy Poem*

This white sheet is shared with you,
and the mystery of finding you,
and the words are all about you,
and worlds appear surrounding you,
cos you have touched my heart.

I want to see all parts of you,
and jump the full moon blues with you,
and feel the come and go of you,
and laugh and cry and dance with you,
and find my way through life with you,
cos you have touched my heart.

# *Trusting*

He lay dozing
while she padded back & forth
from bedroom to bathroom
bathroom to bed;
toothbrush
dangling from a toothpasty mouth
make-up ready to be wiped away
in preparation for another day.

Lazily drifting his eye
around the familiar contour of her
drowsily aroused
by an unexpected peep
of flesh,
a flash of thigh,
the darker hollow
of an outstretched armpit
reaching to unhook
a delicate layer
of underwear,
and happy to watch her,
not wishing to disturb
the sweet busy-ness of this
night-time routine,
he idly let his hand
slide down beneath the sheets
stroking a trail over and along
the length of his nakedness.

She heard his briefly held intake of breath,
glanced towards the bed,
saw his eyes flicker shut,
his face relax
and the deep moan
of deeper contentment
settle in him;
and she smiled,
from the middle of the room,
happy to have made him happy.

# *From Collette*

Sweet fifteen and never been kissed
flicking pages of a book with drowsy flies,
mocking look, see me standing by the shrub trees,
calling softly, holding my arms to catch
your sandalwood chest,
take deep in my summer molten seas.

In the grass and sand smell the earth of love,
trod mellow with the sun.
I feel your eyes in my thighs and sanguine sighs,
your fresh cream hands innocent in meadows,
I'll sink below to change your Sunday proudness,
your fleecy, lacy, spun pride.

Pretend this is a dream,
let's play tigers blowing red at night
and animals;
boy child sell out, the time has come,
we'll have leaves like pillows
in the hot, shot, shingle dunes.

# Modem Gal

A question popped up on her screen
idly surfing the net one night,
and on a whim
she answered it,
found the it to be a him
and thus began a wooing;
a romance by satellite
CD-Romeo and Juliet,
modem man with modem gal,
the female with her E-male
dot
A blow to virtual reality
yet
who would've thought she'd actually get
a real live lover on the Internet!

## *Therapy*

Love is so elusive to me
like looking for a parrot
in my apple tree.

Where did my knowledge
and instincts go
to lead this life
with nothing to show.

Was I born without a clue,
no handy backpack
of what to do,
no map of myself just an idea
that hurt is all
and so is fear?

I see this day with summer sun
and boots on my new life just begun,
a barbecue lit on a misty night,
a glow abounds and nothing to fight.

But what will it take to learn this way,
a barrage of truths that might not sway
the way I am

so what to do
when the dream you have
might not come true?

## *Semantic Gap*

Teenage Truan with the short, short hair,
rubbing and polishing a bad cut,
'bad, man' means good in his world,
seems a bit short to me,
but I'm only his mum.

# *Serendipity*

Sipping cognac on a rainy day
with a treasured friend in a Paris cafe;
steam misting the panes of glass
outside a blur of colour passed –
windswept arms struggling to regain
control of umbrellas in the driving rain.
The treasured friend had cocked her head
and setting down her glass had said:
'So, what will happen next?'
I'd turned to her a touch perplexed –
'In your life I mean, what kind of man?'
I'd laughed and shrugged 'maybe he'll be an
American'.
She'd leaned forward, cupping her chin,
'ooh!' she'd cooed, 'have you already met him?'
'Oh no my darling, but I dream
of a complete up-ending of everything
and in my dream I see a swing
away from the familiar track:
I see him tall – I see him black!'.


Next stop Dublin, to see some plays,
brilliant crisp autumn days;
Tom Murphy, Congreve, Ibsen and more
and thus it was I met Shakespeare's Moor:
tall, black, a towering Othello
and an absolutely darling fellow!

Next day walking around Dublin Town
retracing a journey of my own
wandering down a familiar street
who do you think that I should meet?
Othello himself, Mr J. Lee. D
all the way from Chicago city!


We shook hands in the sun, hands held tight.
Later, we met again that night –
some food, some wine, a cup of tea –
Oh welcome delicious serendipity!


He moved me on and he moved me on from
the place I needed moving on from.

## *Mask*

'Ooh, don't you look good!', they say,
'Thank you', say I, 'Do I?'
and inside I cry
'No! you don't know!'
'You sound so good!', they say
and inside I die.

How can it be
that I mask so expertly my melancholy?
Why, I cry, when I die every day
can the difference between
what I feel,
what they see
lie
so very separate & awry?

## *Unavailable*

You, your cover-ups and protected heart,
your masked face with spy hole centred small,
through which to glimpse the secret carried
in your knowing look.

I tiptoed close and pressed my eye
against the gap you rose to let me in,
but only saw disdain and worming hate
for those who dared to peep.

# *Exit*

Right
that's it
enough is enough –
you do me wrong.
Breaking
as you do
the code of friendship
you
make a mockery
of everything that I hold true
and
of every single thought,
idea
and gift
of trust
I ever made to
you.

Beware the ancient proverb:
He it is
that seeks only to contemplate himself
slips on the dung pile in his path
and enters not the sacred valley
of enlightenment
for he is blind.

And Screw you too.

## *High Tea*

I have this fancy for you both,
the one to bring me cream
the other tea,
a royal blend to serve my fantasy,
a balanced choice of you plus him.

I'll make a sandwich of myself
to be of tasty crumbs,
stuff myself till I am blown
and floating like a glass.
This way I'll feel no loss,
no ache for him that seems
so grassy greener.

But such is man – so awfully mean
– if I forgot and half asleep
should speak aloud the wrong man s name,
then oh so hoity,
you'd both leave the restaurant
bill unpaid,
and that would be the end of it.

# Bedtime

We'll get a six foot bed, he said.
      A six foot bed! A six foot bed!
Of course it makes no difference if the love has
gone dead,
      if the love has gone dead, if the love has
      gone dead...
But they didn't know then so they bought the bed
      the six foot bed, the six foot bed,
and they laid it all out, wooden planks & frame,
      six foot planks, six foot planks,
and they put it together with hammer & screws,
and threw themselves on the thin mattress of foam
      to christen the bed, the six foot bed...
And then she rolled over to the left
And he rolled over to the right,
and that's how they spent the rest of the night
      the rest of the night, the rest of the night
and the weeks & the months & the years to come
either side of the great divide further & further apart.

We'll get a five foot bed! She said.
      A five foot bed? A five foot bed...
with a lovely deep mattress & a proper sprung base,
a proper sprung base, a proper sprung base.

So they dismantled the frame of the six foot bed;
stacked the wood in the cellar with the mattress of
foam,
and they bought a smaller five foot bed –
but it was all too late by then, too late.
Eventually they had to separate.

Time went by
and then she decided to get rid of the bed
        the six foot bed, the six foot bed;
She dragged the foam mattress out onto a skip
but a gale force wind came up in the night
and snatched it up into the air,
blowing it here, buffeting it there
so that when the skip was taken away
the snow sodden mattress still lay in the street,
mocking memory of her defeat rotting in the gutter
        in the gutter, in the gutter,
and to her absolute dismay
there it stayed for several days
till, thank God, the council were called
& at last they took the sodding thing away.

She sleeps well now all alone
secure in the comfort of the five foot bed
        the five foot bed, the five foot bed,
and it really is a very good bed & all of her very own!

## *After The Interview For A Job*

I can't take no more rejection
it's mucking up my head,
is it my looks or something I said?
I know — I'm too short, no, no, too tall.
Maybe in another life i did a bad thing
and am paying the price for a gory killing.
Is my voice unattractive do I speak with a lisp?
but it's soft and it's lovely, Ah I see it's too crisp.
Oh bother this job, this silly acting lark,
Mr Coward was right, don't put your daughter...
                                        but hark!
Is that the phone I hear ringing, perhaps it's for me?
Yes it is! Yes it is! Yes it is! It is she.
Of course I would *love* to, anything you say,
just to hear that applause and be in a play.

How much are they paying, Oh no this is farce
you can tell then to stick it right up their... ask
me again later, I'm sure we'll agree,
It's 'creating' that counts and not just the fee,
because they want 'me',
they want *me*,
they want *me*.

Are you sure they want *me*?

## *Short Love Poem*

I am between the tulip leaves
held by the passion of your love.
Van Morrison sang, 'so quiet in here'
so quiet to be all pink
and swishy with tulips.

# *Hotel*

On the edge of the bed they sat
she too thin – he too fat;
in his hands he held his head
sitting on the hotel bed.
Barely an hour since they'd met,
weekend case unopened yet..
She, sat staring into space
no emotion on her face
muscles in her neck stretched taut,
arms crossed to give support
to the shaking of her hand;
twisting round the wedding band
that she knew she still must wear
but she could no longer bear.

Outside their room in the corridor
footsteps approached then passed their door.
She half turned now to look at him.
He raised his head, his expression grim,
both his hands clenched in a fist.
Stroking her fingers along his wrist
it shocked her as she felt him tense
against her and a mounting sense
of fear rose in her heart
dreading the moment they'd have to part.

Not a word had yet been spoken
the silence in the room unbroken
but for the creaks of an old hotel
and the rain still pounding on the window cill.

For over a year they'd met this way
driving miles whenever they
could snatch a night or day alone.
This morning though from his car phone
she'd sounded slightly strained, he'd thought,
and in his rear-view mirror caught
reflected there, the clench of his jaw
and a look in his eye not seen before.

When he'd arrived at their meeting place
and seen the pinched look on her face –
her long sleek hair pulled back too tight,
gathered at the nape shot through with white,
her features etched in stark relief –
he'd stared at her in disbelief.
Then suddenly she was transformed again,
her smile dissolving all the strain
and reaching up for a longed for kiss
winked at him as her lips touched his.

Still smiling in his car she'd said
she longed to get him into bed!
Then suddenly she had begun to cry.
But when he'd stopped to ask her why,
she'd sunk down deep into her seat
head dipped so that she couldn't meet
the mass of questions in his eyes –
determined not to tell him lies,
desperate that he'd understand;
trying to remember all she'd planned
to say when the time came;
hoping that he wouldn't blame
her too much for the pain ahead.

Yet – 'Please forgive me' was all she'd said.

The skin on his face was blazing hot

'What are you talking about, for what?',
'Tell me, Jesus, what do you mean?',

His hands were clammy, he thought he'd scream
but his voice got strangled in his throat
and muffled in the collar of his overcoat.

'It's over my love', he'd heard her say,
'I love you love, but I can't stay
with you today – or anymore.'

He'd shut off the engine, opened his door
got out of the car and started to run.
Just then the lightning had begun.
She'd got out too to call him back
terrified he might get struck.

He'd run for cover under the trees
but as she'd started to follow, her knees
had buckled beneath her, and she'd knelt
crumpled beside the car and felt
so alone and so unhappy.
Back in the car she'd turned the key –
her stockings were torn, she was soaking wet –
she'd thrown the shift into 'Drive' and set
the windscreen wipers flying,
peering through the rain and trying
to catch sight of him on the way
to the little hotel where they'd always stay.

At reception they said that he
had already checked in and taken the key.
She'd walked up to the second floor
and from the landing could see their door –
pausing briefly for time to think,

wondering if he'd have had a drink
by then and what his mood might be,
she'd turned the handle and pushed gently.

Inside, a bottle of gin – half gone;
from the bathroom the sound of the shower full on;
his rain soaked coat draped over a chair,
the rest of his clothes slung any-old-where;
and just outside the bathroom door
his lighter and cigarettes on the floor –
funny, silly habit he had
and one of the things that had driven her mad
ever since they'd begun their affair
but now reassured her that he really was there...
She'd lit one herself as she hung up her coat.
The harsh tobacco had caught in her throat
choking her so that she'd started to cough
just as she'd heard the taps turned off –
she'd sat, eyes closed in the darkening room
feeling cold and sick in the gathering gloom –
she'd heard the door of the bathroom click
and opened her eyes to see him flick
the light switch on above the bed.

His thinning hair lay damp on his head;
with chest and shoulders still gleaming wet,
lighter snapping on his cigarette,
his bath towel wound around his waist,
he'd moved with that peculiar grace
so often found in very large men,
crossing the room to the bottle and then
pouring himself a very large shot
hoping the shock would dull the knot
of sickening pain that hung, unbidden,
quivering there deep within him.

53

He'd noticed the case she'd remembered to bring
in from the car with everything
he'd need before he could leave.
He'd looked at her then and couldn't believe
that this might be the last time he'd see
the rise of her neck, the slope of her knee –
too desolate now to ask her why –
and suddenly he'd begun to cry
He'd sat, his head held in his hands,
in despair that all his plans
all his hopes and dreams were gone.
Nothing at all now to be done.

Outside the room in the corridor
footsteps approached then passed their door.
He raised his head, his expression grim
aware that she had turned to him.
Her long cool fingers touched his wrist,
his hand was bunched into a fist –
he looked her in the face and then
he hit her again and again and again.

On the edge of the bed they sat
she too thin – he too fat.
Barely an hour since they'd met,
weekend case unopened yet.
Not a word had yet been spoken
the silence in the room unbroken
but for the creaks of an old hotel
and the rain still pounding on the window cill.

## Guilt

My sinful ways
have let me stray
from what I'm taught
and ought to be.

Oh women only can be true
to what she is,
and have the luck
to wed a man
she wants to fuck.

## Feeling A Bit Down

Bloody Cornwall,
bloody granite,
bloody Cornwall,
bloody sea,
bloody sand smells,
bloody rocks,
bloody life boat,
bloody fish market,
bloody methodists,
bloody primary school.

Bloody London,
bloody no air,
bloody no God,
bloody no sea,
bloody no life.

Bloody Cornwall.

## Down Under D-Day

I had to make my way
over to the fringes
to see
how far away
from the centre they were –
I got lost.
Too far.
I try to return to the centre
to try to make sense of the whole
I thought I was closer
than I am
but when I look over my
shoulder
to right, to left
I see a desert –
I want to run
but have no clue which way –
no landmarks
to guide me
no flower blooming in the bleached out sand
no blade of grass –
arid
empty
no wind
no sound
no sign of any hope at all.

# Devotion

The dwarf came early to church,
and shuffled from gate to locked gate
pushing to get in.
Eventually, because it was raining,
he ignored the people staring from
the restaurant across the street,
and sang a hymn
while peeing in the gutter.

## *Another Sighting*

No more tears will I weep over you.

No, you are not dead to me
you never could be,
but
however eager the spring of your step or
the gleam of your eye in welcome handshake,
the spread of your shell
overhangs a shallow well
and the reflection there disappoints…

No, no more tears for you.

# *Survival*

When you left,
your love for me running down
like blood between my legs,
you said no more.
But now you know I'm loved again
and in your once contented room
you say more sorry's than you've done before.

I'm not laughing
to hear you cry,
or saying, I told you so,
I'm resting in a space
beneath the floor,
hiding in the darkness we maintained
until it's safe,
like a mouse waiting
to feel sure
the cat has got bored.

# Breaking Off

Everything in London right now lovie is sheer hell,
the work as well –
a nightmare, I'm in despair
so what more can I tell you sweetie
except that in this really awful state
the need to communicate
is just too great to wait such a very,very long wait.
So darling, duckie,lovie, dear
maybe I wasn't altogether clear
      you say potato/I say potato
      you say tomato/I say tomato

I thought it worth a try
but I'm on reserve tank only now and it's nearly dry
and the reality is that I
am far too fragile & depressed
to sustain the emotional tie
I so want with you
but which saps my energy and my time too
and upon which I can't rely.

I give in admit defeat;
what my head thought possible my heart proves
wrong
so regretfully, as they say in the song,
Let's call the whole thing off.

Take care,
Good Luck,
So long.

# The Trip

We passed the frigate on the starboard side
sailing up the Tamar,
and my father from his grave – while halfway
through his Cornish jig of joy – yelled
'that's my girl' as we ploughed the wind to Plymouth,
and the war ships, grey dead men sat silent at the jetty,
called Battle Axe, Sea Dog, Brazen and Campbell
                                        Town,
and submarines, redundant, and surprisingly for sale.

The ghost of my father stowed away beside me
saluted his navy hat,
for he saw differently than I,
when Plymouth was a firework, a furnace in the sky,
and bombs fell daily where destroyers lay,
and the girls kissed sailors
returning safely up the sound.

# *Traveller*

I think of you
this morning
as you pack up,
lock up,
park the car,
take to the air;
I wonder how you are
wonder how you'll be
wonder what wonders of the world you'll see
and I envy you
escaping the whole christmas hullabaloo;
jangled nerves,
driven to be jolly;
the lists, the plans
the supermarket trolley
a dead weight of stuff to stuff into
another bit of another day of yet another year;
and I envy you
knowing how little to pack,
the priority mouth organ & typewriter
in your economy size ruck-sack
tucked in with the T-shirts on your back;
and I envy you the chutzpah
of the way you pick your way through a day.

I look up into a sky of dull
and wave at nothing
wishing you Bon Voyage
Big time!

# Hollywood Dream

A great big cat sits on the mat
watching it's garden grow –
sitting at the window surveying the rain,
damp muddy paw marks on counterpane,
guardian magnificent of the family home,
it waits to be served it's dinner.

In another time and long ago
its mistress took a flight through
what seemed an endless night
stretching out over beyond time,
pitch black,no sight of sun
only tinkle of vodka glass
and familiar aroma of Gauloises (or was it Gitanes?)

Setting her chic elegant ankled black suede boot
upon Los Angelean sand,
blonde hair caught in the desert wind,
radiant in the sunshine of Tinsel Town,
how could she know that somewhere downtown
danger lurked
ready to undermine
the gorgeous pink and pale grey cashmere line of her,
the cameo and pearl?

Stepping over
the invisible line of Make-Believe,
past Yucca, Palm and rose Stucco
in silver Mustang,
beneath the neon hoardings,

clapboard facade
all that separates the wild coyote
from suntanned Manhattan-sipping Californian
in celluloid land,
no sense had she that treachery
lay in the cool shadow of the Cypress tree –
betrayal in silence, exile, cunning…
whilst all around her sunning themselves,
glittering with rainbow coloured halos
above their lovely heads,
the Tinsel Towners
dazzled.

Razzle dazzle splintered images
scattered in the dust…
showbiz…
The storm gathered.
The sun vanished
the rain that fell washed part of California away
slipping, sliding into the ocean
as she made her getaway
as she returned to plundered dreams of Islington N1.

And all this, of course, long, long before
the cat was e 'er a twinkle in it's daddy's eye…
yet possessed of that great wisdom only known to cats
surveying it's Mistress now across the kitchen floor
it winks it's almond eye
taps it's nose with it's great paw
and says: 'But Mary, Mary, sometimes contrary,
just look how bloody marvellous your garden now
doth grow!'

## For Sean (age 5) from Peru

There's a candy floss sky
and a peppermint moon,
and the blue of the night
is very blue
in Peru.

There's a mayor in the town
where the cars go round,
 but not past his house,
he's sleeping.
And in the morning at two
the electricity stops
in Peru.

There's a road made of mud
where the babies and dogs
play with mangoes and ice
and the boats float by
with bananas piled high,
and everything new
is old
in Peru.

## *Notting Hill Gate Day*

The troubles don't hurt the carnival any more.
the policeman have flowered hats
and boogie down the grove cupping
small, brown faces in their hands.
Madeleine Bell's melting pot sings out,
swirling mixing like a chocolate ripple cream.
I wear a badge, it says, Black Smile Day 92,
eat Japanese rice balls, sugar cane peeled by machete,
Dragon Stout sent from the Caribbean.
A Trocaderon rain dance reggaes past
with fringed umbrellas
dripping like antimacassars on a carousel,
trucks full of Bob Marleys,
and feathered, black haired women,
moving as synchronised swimmers, lazily wanton.
An Australian clasps tight an African's hand,
macho in it's touching.

Black smile Day '92
no night of knives,
no day of blood,
no TV footage for the news.
They said,
the carnival was so peaceful
next year it will be held in Soweto.

## The Pretender

So Smug
so self opinionated
so absolutely sure –
pompous little bore
in his vacuum packed Action Man case;
nasty neo-Nazi notions neatly stacked in place,
ready to slot in, slot out and re-invent
without a trace of truth;
a telling pout
hiding behind the hired hooligan mask
of the Lager Lout –
ruling by the tool – good God, what kind of fool
does he take us for…?
Big Mac machismo, whip crack snapping at the ankle
of anything that threatens to give the lie
to the bogus Old Boy network, the Old School tie.
No! No, it simply will not do
to trivialise,
to minimise,
to strut and trample underfoot all suspicion of the new,
wearing his ignorance with pride
a sling of arrows at his side,
their poisoned tips poised to strip
the leaf of it's green, the sky of it's blue.
Knock! Knock! Who's there? So puffed up, so secure.
But pierce the vacuum seal and pfuff…fff
the air escapes
deflates, disintegrates -
No sign now of Action Man – no, not even Barbie Doll!–
empty, void, nothing –
no-one there at all.

# Warning

Watch out!
Don't get too close
She was born
with an extra vein
Lime drips through
and it can stain you!

Watch out!
Don't kiss
an arsenal of knives
with poisoned tips
lie behind the lips
and they could slay you.

## *An Actor I Knew*

On a good day,
posed perfectly on the edge,
his strong leg has placed his foot
quite firmly this side of hell
and justly flows the warmth and wit
cajoling us to curl about him.

But when it's bad,
he looses his balance
and tips into that black hole
where no one goes with reason.
Pale and glowering and nervous as
a cat's whisker he could
attack without warning.

You do not want to face him in a duel,
(especially on a stage).

# *Nightmare*

Nerves out on stalks
straggly
dead white –
I twist my head
and from the corner of my eye
espy
the weed sprouting from my heel
lime green weed
sticking through my stocking –
I tug at it in horror
 but it won't budge
burrowed deep in flesh
 its shoot stronger than its host,
I open my mouth to scream
because I suppose I must be dying

## *Satiated*

Someone touched me,
felt the ferns growing
deeply in my brain,
grubbed around squeezing
my flesh, rolling it between
his fingers.
Took a straw and sucked
the deep juices raw from
my bones,
drained away my tears
in a flood of ecstasy,
so now I cannot cry
at sad movies and
Walt Disney.

## A Girl I Knew

You are too pale for life
You are mimeographed between
Victorian pages
a citron pressed flower.

You have never smelt
sex on sheets,
you have never known
the ache of longing,
the faded skeleton of a priest
lurks happily in your soul.

Someday, like a television set,
you will reduce to a clear, bright
central spot
and extinguish yourself

# Nuala of the North

'Hold me', she whimpered,
I haven't enough arms to hold me,
enough men to hold me –
Hold me!' she said.
And they flock, these men,
they run to her
scattering each other this way and that
to be there
for her –
not only men but women too
rushing to protect
their little girl
their little pretty
Nuala of the north,
who winds them around her,
slipping her dimpled arms
into the different garments
that these different people
are for her.
Doe-eyed, seductively intense
and – so they say – apparently quite guileless
in the many guises she adopts
to cloak her self deceiving,
so self absorbed is she
that when she twists and turns her version
of what's real, what's true,
no-one dares to question it
in case their little darling falls askew.

Hovering at the edge of the pool
swaying slightly in the heat

she swivels those tremendous bovine eyes
to make quite sure
that all who watch her with baited breath,
are agonisingly unsure which way she'll fall—
poised
they are ready to lay down
all
for her
slave to her merest whim.
She lifts her chubby cherubic arm above her lovely
head,
above her luscious locks her gleaming comb glints
its brilliant teeth sharp and treacherous;
the shell like hand that grasps it
set in a fist of steel,
its grip
a vice
on the life that she so ruthlessly
yet so sweetly fashions
as she bends it
inexorably
to her will.

Well, well, well…
What a clever little thing,
clever little girl
clever little Nuala –
Nuala of the North.

# Burglary

All in the name of Love,
she said;
and then pulled off the neatest cheat
by stealing the carpet from under his feet;
took coffee table, kitchen chair;
she stripped the bloody bedroom bare,
ripped out the shelving in the hall,
and all the pictures from the wall

Microwave gone
curtains too
even the screwdriver
that screwed out the screws
of ornament and looking glass,
mirror witness to this theft,
Passport, certificates of birth
all removed in the name of Love.

No kettle even for a cup of tea
just a sofa, a bed
a chest, a TV
and on the floor the answerphone
stark remains of what had been home -
all the doors left ajar
their iron doorstops also gone
and all in the name of…

I LOVE YOU, she said
in the message she'd left…
What tears had she shed
as she packed up
the duvet and sheets from the bed?
Why she even took the toilet roll too!
And all in the name of love,
did she say?
Well hey, lady Love,
Fuck you.

## *Thoughts on a Tube*

I often wonder if
we'll make it
out of the scrum
that was there
when we met –
I'd hoped for peace
this time –
only to find
the game goes on
into infinity
with no injury
time allowed.

Ah well,
is it really the playing
and not the winning? –
So bingo,
you've suddenly
grown old together…

## *Stage Fright*

Tom Stoppard sat on a small wooden chair,
just call me 'TS' he said,
and threw back his cloak with his long dark hair,
there in that theatre
in the day theatre light,
and all I could do was stare and stare.

l built this play with bricks he said
just like a child's plaything,
one colour on colour certainly lead
to this scene we are going to do,
 let's read out loud so you can hear,
and the words spun slick in his handsome head.


We were rapt in a circle so secure
the tumble of words made me numb,
smelted and smoothed and always sure
served hot from the oven
for us to conceal,
there in that theatre
in the day theatre light,
and all 1 could feel was fear and fear.

## The Cure

Time passed.
I didn't call.
Nor did he.
And suddenly
I found it didn't matter after all.
Eureka!
I'm cured!

## Sick

I'm sick
I'm sick of dying
for a pair of arms
to hold me
lips to kiss
and a sweet heart
to give my friendship
and all my loving to.

So where the fuck ARE you?

## *Letter From Spain*

Will you always love me?
Sitting bubble-gummed in pleasure
in your English room
beneath a window full of blown
Forget-me-nots.

I will spend my days wishing
in northern chords,
and the sea will hear me cry out
because I want you so much in the middle
I have to drink a glass of water, dark,
in the early hours, to cool,
I'm as the fighter before a fight,
picking at oranges,
nervously waiting,
fiddling with rings
and frantically dying with
your love inside
they ought to operate.

The sand is yellow today
as I look out towards their
no parking zone.
Yellow, moth flown, hazy days,
where I can sip a Fanta, cold,
and love the French women, browned,
because they are more beautiful than I.
Did you know there is no tide at all,
and the horses are fly ridden thin
from dawn to tea time,

although there is no tea,
I've looked.

I fancied an ice cream and a tall
Italian waiter serving coffee on a
black tray,
swaying to an old Beatles tune
which catches time if nothing else.
There is a band but I cannot jive.

I fell in the swimming pool,
I was drunk,
down in the wiggly depths of plastic blue,
I saw myself drown.
But I was on a windy marsh, and the grass was
aching in the curlewed wind.

## *Meeting in the Street*

– Well, doubtless we'll be in touch –
said you
– please do –
was my reply
and our eyes
locked for just long enough
to see the strain
and the pain
and still I don't know why.

## *Dylan Thomas and the Mermaid of Zennor*

Who is it that would comb her streaming hair
with dark carved lily teeth?
Only the mermaid calling melancholic from the cove,
blowing through deep water coils,
reverberating in the spongy hills.

And Dylan, unprepared,
drunkenly one day in Zennor,
up to his eyes in pinks and pathos,
heard the mermaid's lament
full of Celtic cries and lost amour,
so tangled by starfish weeds.

Lured down to the sands,
he stood bewitched before the sunken siren,
and finally,
drowned his sorrows in a sea of words.

# Nostalgia

Looking backwards can be fun,
but sometimes,
while probing an old diary,
or prodding a faded print,
the past becomes unbearable
and like a grumpy child
is best left alone.

## *Goodbye-Hello*

Bidding farewell
to a dear friend
snatched from life too soon –
a chance glance
across the kirk
meets the eye of a sweet soul,
with whom,
oh, so very many years ago,
I briefly shared some precious time.
But then, so out of love with me was I,
gnashing angry little teeth,
biting into each & every day,
too afraid to stop
stand still, take stock;
to really touch
to look & feel,
and placing no value upon myself
I couldn't value him.
Callow youth, so cavalier.
But in these rum & sometimes calmer
middle years,
the twinkling & the winking of his eye
is welcome, welcome.
Later at dusk, alone again,
I think of him at the wake & smile,
so glad on this bleak day of grief
to have brushed my lips upon his cheek
and felt his lips on mine.

## The Finding

My visit was brief
our shadows met
and kissed
held tight the
blood between us
lost in my childhood.

I saw you hold your palm
across my eyes
to soothe away
my headache.
If you remembered
I left too soon
to ask.

# Friendship

In these dreadful times
of loss and pain,
friendship,
or what remains of it,
might be all there is
to turn to;
and if that too seems to fail
we rail
against the isolation of our misery
unable to
make sense
of silence.

No-one ever said it would be easy;
but
if there 's any point at all –
and often that's thrown hopelessly in doubt –
don't we ignore
the flutter of a friendly wave
that might soothe
or even save
or simply say – Hello –
at our peril?

## *July 1992*

The tears for Janet
flow soft and free
like a sad ballet
or the drowning
of a butterfly.
My friend will soon be gone.
Once again the preciousness of time
turns summersaults
lands on it's feet laughing,
I want to put a pie in it's face.
I wish i'd seen her again,
I wish I'd said I love you,
I wish I'd
I wish I'd,
I wish
I,
I...

## Trojan Women

Striding with Hecuba
along Killiney Beach
heads swathed
dipped low
pitching the weight
of themselves
into
the wind and rain –
Amazons three
roaring their mirth
their agony
over the bellow of the sea –
moving as one
immense –
muscles straining
on the shifting sand –
hurling
shoulder and breast
against
The Wall of Troy
across The Irish Sea.

# *Eire*

Driving hard
in the driving rain
on the Belfast road
from Dundalk
through Drogheda & Balbriggan
to Dublin's fair city;
eyes still itching
with too little sleep,
sluggish mind inching its way
around the start of the day;
the heart aching, uncertain,
preparing for another farewell,
a little shaky,
a little anxiety beginning to take a hold
of things beyond control –
delays – forgotten belongings – & so on.
I shift my weight behind the wheel of the car
and take a sidelong glance
at my dear sweet friend
Eve,
sitting low in her seat beside me,
her little dog in her lap
her ravishing deep black eyes sweeping
over the sodden green countryside,
and I want to hold her very, very tight;
what journeys we've travelled she & I,
what pits of hell we've neared & saved each other
from
over so many years.
Along side one another now,

me driving her in her car
sharing the burden of the long airport drive,
only the windscreen wipers thudding
across & across to break the silence,
briefly caught up in our separate thoughts,
until some wicked almost forgotten bit of news
has us laughing again
laughing & laughing
teasing it back & forth in the unravelling,
stretching, slightly re-shaping it
in the putting it back together again: –
she,
tender & wise and so funny so wonderfully funny –
my God! how we have laughed
for twenty years or more;
and now we look – with some trepidation –
into the second part of our lives;
she,
having changed course, leaving England
successful in her business here
back in her home town
small provincial border town
people on first name terms
witness to each others lives,
praising & censorious by turns;
groups of men philosophising over a jar
setting the world to rights;
women shopping
popping in to get a hair wash & a trim;
windows of bars & hairdressers
steamed up with all the local gossip!
Eve's salon too –
a stream of housewives mothers, children,
Brides to be;

make-ups,
waxings,
legs & lips
and varnishing of finger tips;
a place to confide
transported briefly from the humdrum;
pampering to please and to be pleased.
And Eve,
giving always giving, living
closely in the bosom of her family
still rooted in its home town,
triumphant in her achievement & success.
Only in bleaker mood, trapped from time to time
positive turned briefly negative,
might it appear an endless path
narrow and empty stretching as far as the eye can
see.
But Eve shakes her fist at dull,
tests herself against the boredom of routine,
and in precious leisure hours
upends the sameness of each working day
reaching into herself through art,
restoring Eve the actress to the stage again;
ever England's loss but Dundalk's gain.

And as for me
an urban child, pure NW3
yet oddly rootless– a great hotchpotch
part middle European, Jewish, Celt –
I am somehow without
the very,very strong identity
I feel so powerfully In Ireland
in Eve s country
in Eve,

and Eve's family.
The truth is that Ireland feels like a home to me.
Profoundly powerful emotions have been stirred in
me,
an invisible thread catching me up in its elaborate
lacework.
Is it safety net or web
I wonder?
Yes, I wonder at it.

Twenty years or so ago
I felt
I think
a kind of threat in the embrace of this island – Ireland;
uncertain of it, unnerved,
excluded by the brilliant double-edged wit;
unpredictable, volatile,
invisible weapons ever at the ready –
or so it seemed –
to stab one in the back.

Older, wiser maybe,
I feel now that the kiss that greets my cheek is warm;
the hand outstretched, firm,
the welcome true
and I find I yearn
for the human scale of this lovely land –
dramatic hills dark & purple
never more than an hours drive away
always faintly looming through the mists;
immense skies sometimes grey & blank with rain,
as now,
as often brilliant blue and sparkingly clear;
a gigantic cyclorama

framing the history, the myths,
the music
the pipe
the drum –
subterranean
resonating deep in bog and ancient rock
and now in the hollow of me;
the magic, the mystery –
I miss it dreadfully
and I'm shocked by how much
the leaving of its people
pierces me.

SUSAN PENHALIGON

# Woman Outside Marks And Spencer's

I am a living poem
walking the streets, Belfast.
Who will buy these ruby words
to wrap around
their garbled tongues
refresh a cake dry memory.

My son, my son
they killed my son
they killed him with
an army gun.

And I am doomed to walk
this shopping mall
with words across my back
and breasts,
a protest shooting through
the elfin soldiers who pass
me neck a neck
and make believe
that l am mad.

## *From Australia*

And how am I here?
Some swift song is flying.
I had flight failure
at Heathrow,
my wings jammed on leaving you.

Diminished in this unknown room,
vacuumed and sanitised for my
own protection,
assuredly no yesterdays germs
stalking my bed.
I wish I'd brought a germ
from you,
that would be something.

I left the smell of your shirts
at Bahrain,
the feel of your skin at
Singapore,
the sound of your voice is
throttled by a telephone cord,
I am turbulent with nightmares.

## Love & The Parasite

I laid it out –
stretched the whole damn thing
out –
had a good look –
a good long look
at it –
thought I could see
all points
North, South, East & West of it –
thought that by pinning it out
I could put it down,
have control of it:
but what I couldn't see
was the tiny worm of hope
sat fat & blind within me:
I wonder that the drip, drip acid
of my pain
does not poison it,
but surely while this tormenting and pointless
love of mine
has life
the wretched worm lives on.

# *Sara*

Sad Sara
Spawning forth
her lost, love story,
sitting in a darkening, doleful room.
I heard the chrysalis cries
of a new experience and you'll
pull through, I said,
as I watched her movie
moving before my eyes,
sunk in her captivating melancholy
with my own remembrances.

# *Trust*

When he did not phone
for a moment
she touched that grief again,
wandering myopically
she crossed the border
to a place of broken glass
and wrenching stomach
and short sharp breaths
and lonely unloved mornings
blinded to the sunlight on a hot day.

Gripped by this arrival
she feared for her sanity,
having done so well
for so many years
and mused how easily
and slippery it was,
how imperceptibly she'd capitulated.

But then he rang
 and covered her in grace
and the world was not toppled
and the oily dragon retreated
to it's gummed up hole,
surprised it had been let out.
She cleaned the house contentedly
and the Laburnum tree
turned razzamatazz yellow
in the London rain.

## Moving On

Come on!
says she,
it's in your gift to lift your hand and wave –
but he
keeps silent
arm fixed by his side,
all that could be celebrated hidden and denied
until
the inevitable moment of surprise
an accidental meeting
and the eyes that greet
shine, smile
grateful at last to have a chance
to meet
shake hands
chat a while –
a sudden rush bubbles up,
fizzes through top to toe;
the tight sprung coil released,
uncurls
unfurls
brushes the outside edges of the smile
with unexpected threat of tears -
not of grief, but welcome relief;
the breath had been held for too long.

Free now to move on.

# The Wall

We're in the dark days now,
my mother, forgetful of the words just spoken,
losing the house where her daughter lives
on her way back from the paper shop
wearing the camel coat I gave her,
shortened now, because she's shrunk
with age and dampened bones,
the power to hurt us all
is all forgiven in her frailty,
although the angles still are sharp -
selfishness comes easy to the single heart.

I watch her dimming eyes
protected by the wall I built between us years ago–
it's well intact and crystallised with adult fear.
I wonder what to do when finally she goes,
there is no time or inclination to knock it down.

# *Knowing*

I know I feel –
and somewhere
deep within
I feel I know.
I think…

I know I feel.

## *Not Quite a Sonnet*

He tripped on a bit of magic
that through some random fusion of his DNA
got lodged in his smile.
And all that felt his allurement were full of wit
and cared far more for things of beauty –
like catkins in a jar just picked
and a sundown body on a bleached out beach.
although he had a sardonic eye that V signed every
                                             vanity,
his handsome face beamed out with crazy love…

to give.

SARA KESTELMAN

## A Dish of Fruit

The tray lay by the hospital bed:
some soup, some fish;
a little white dish of syruped fruit,
peeled, sectioned,
pink & glazed & gleaming in the shallow bowl.
I asked:

'What's that, do you think?'

A little dazed my friend looked at the dish,
looked for some time, then said:
'I don't know, do I?'

Was there a hint of a smile on his lips?
I couldn't be certain, couldn't be sure
and so, afraid to ruffle him more,
afraid to laugh, or even smile
just in case, as had happened before,
he thought that I was trivialising;
not understanding, not kind, not reliable after all –
I paused... then said:

'I wonder if they're plums?'

He turned to me, an odd look in his eye.
Puzzled was he? Or was it confusion or irritation
maybe?

'I don't know, how should I know?'
he said to me again.

106

And then, he reached into the bowl
and popped a piece of fruit into his mouth –
he chuckled & grinned:

'Yes', he said with some delight,
'it's a kind of fruit, I think you' re right'.

We took the tray into another room to sit him at a
table
and went in search of ketchup & brown sauce.
He ate the fish, the croquette potatoes
the broccoli hungrily,
and every now & then added to a mouthful
 a forkful of the fruit.
He appeared not to notice,
or maybe, it was a culinary success,
and he simply didn't tell me!
Maybe I should try it for myself and see.

Dear, sweet friend, plagued by anxiety
convinced that everybody
must either think that he was mad
or not quite mad enough.

And then an unexpected discovery:
in passing, as it were accidentally,
a friend happened to say
a word to him,
a word he could identify
and comprehend;
a word that framed, gave focus to his state,
a word that allowed him to separate

and isolate his experience
from what had seemed to be
a snake pit in his mind;
a word that might have terrified
but instead clarified
everything for him.
And this word, this single word
'dementia'
illuminated him,
restored his grace,
his dignity,
his clarity of thought;
freed him to give voice,
to crystallise;
to re-assess, re-balance
his fear,
even as he slipped in and out of it,
with a kind of gravity and calm.
Anger replaced by insight;
apprehension by comprehension:
The Lunatic, The Lover & The Poet,
Theseus
mounting guard
a blaze of light
at the outside edges of the forest.

# *For Angel*

Remember Angel
before the black death
caught him,
on my wall in a photograph.
Remember Angel
before the virus
got him,
standing by me
in the house by the sea
this gentle friend
who did no harm
smiles coyly at the lens,
framed on my wall forever.

Impossible to judge
or say, it's only them,
as Satan would have liked.
Retribution for that kind of love
is not a becoming thought
when you have
a dead Angel on your wall.

# *Publishing*

It's a 114 pages
they say,
but really it's 98
you see
cos 14 of these
are already used up
with the blank page & title & contents & such…
so precisely how much
of the work can be used
is then counted & reworked & borrowed & squeezed
into 29 lines to a page
so they say…
so you lay it all out,
go back to the start
taking the whole numbers thing apart –
forget about art –
tear out your hair,
chuck the whole bloody book in the air
and just when you think you can't take any more
someone mentions the magic of 34
and sure enough, there's a precedent too
and several poets & publishers who
prefer to lay out the page this way
so you take up yet another day
until at last you've got it fixed
all the cutting & juggling & matching mixed,
and you clip it together to have a last look
and wonder of wonders,
you've got a book!